D0878431

A Gift for: _____

From: _____

WALKTHETALK.COM

Resources for Personal and Professional Success

Live Inspired

The WALK THE TALK Company
1100 Parker Square, Suite 250
Flower Mound, Texas 75028
972.899.8300

WALK THE TALK books may be purchased for educational, business, or sales promotion use.

WALK THE TALK® and The WALK THE TALK® Company are registered trademarks of
Performance Systems Corporation.

Live Inspired™ is a trademark of Michelle Sedas.

Printed in the United States of America
10 9 8 7 6 5 4 3 2 1

Designed by Sandra Beddow
Printed by Branch-Smith

$12.95

ISBN-10:   1-935537-58-X
ISBN-13: 978-1-935537-58-8

51295>

LIVE
Inspired

BY MICHELLE SEDAS

This book is dedicated to the
Inspired Living Cafe community.

You inspire me.

TABLE OF CONTENTS

INTRODUCTION

Live Inspired is truly a community work. In late 2008, after months of preparation, WalkTheTalk.com unveiled the Inspired Living Cafe, a virtual oasis amidst the hustle and bustle of daily life. Here, our goal is to stretch your mind, gladden your heart, and nourish your soul. As the host of the Inspired Living Cafe, I write about what's inspiring me. Spotlighting new books and stand-out authors, the Inspired Living Cafe has become a destination for inspiration.

Wanting to write a book on the idea of *living inspired*, I began by researching quotes and reading books on inspiration. I asked a few of my friends what *living inspired* meant to them. Reading the enthusiasm and joy in their heartfelt responses, I knew that I had hit on a topic that would resonate with readers. After a couple more months of writing, I felt the need to draw upon more sources of inspiration. That's when it came to me: the Inspired Living Cafe has thousands of community members! I wonder how they would define *living inspired*. We then held a contest asking the community to answer the question,

"What does Living Inspired mean to you?" To our delight, we received over 400 submissions to this question from Inspired Living Cafe community members all over the world.

That weekend after the contest, I took a writing retreat. Armed with my over-400 contest emails, a stack of Inspired Living Cafe books for inspiration, plenty of coffee, and my trusty laptop, I set out to write. I did most of my writing in an outdoor gazebo. As if preparing for my arrival, the pear trees lining the walkway out to the gazebo had blossomed only the day before. Listening to the birds sing, feeling the wind move about, sensing the change of seasons in the air, my mind became free of the worries of daily life. It was here, in the heart of serenity, that I read every contest submission. I read poems, dedications to family members, and personal stories of tragedy and triumph. These deep, thought-provoking, touching, and at times humorous words inspired me. You'll find many of these quotes scattered among the pages of this book.

In this life, we can choose to let the burdens of our responsibilities weigh heavily on our shoulders. We can choose to complain about the drudgery of our everyday existence. We can choose to be victims, overwhelmed by our circumstances. Or, we can choose to live inspired! If life is what we choose to make of it, then I will choose a life full of love and laughter; excitement and exhilaration; happiness and hope. I will choose to live inspired! This book is designed to give you the courage to go after your dreams, to live the life you've always imagined, to help you not merely live, but to *Live Inspired!*

Since we are each on a different path, working toward different goals, and through different circumstances, it's up to you to decide exactly what *living inspired* means to you. At the end of each chapter, you'll have an opportunity to reflect back upon what you just read. Make this book yours. Allow your own unique experiences, thoughts, and feelings to shine through.

Now, it's time to enjoy this journey together as we discover what it means to *live inspired*. So now grab a pen, kick off your shoes, and relax. Envision the sound of the birds singing as well as the sight of scenic surroundings. Open your mind as well as your imagination. Let the weight of the world fall to the wayside as we explore new thoughts and ideas together.

Let the journey begin!

Michelle Sedas

Living inspired

is born in the awareness that this is it!

We have one chance at life.

And the wonderful gift

we are given every morning

is the choice of how we are going to live that moment,

that day.

Sally Cofer-Lindberg

Modesto, California

LIVE INSPIRED: THE POEM

LIVE INSPIRED

In the darkness, late last night,
I had a remarkable dream.
There I was, walking around town,
when I discovered a recurring theme.

I noticed that the sky was gray.
The landscape lacked all color.
Here the days were exactly alike:
Just one after another...after another.

I saw many of my family and friends.
In their faces the same looks I found:
Lackluster, melancholy, vacant eyes,
and they all stared at the ground.

When I awoke I ran outside
and lifted my hands to the skies.
Thankful to live in this world
where vivid colors flood my eyes.

A place where life has purpose and meaning
and tiny miracles are all around.
A world where true, rich friendships
are just waiting to be found.

So today, I've awakened to the idea
that in this life I am free
to become the person deep inside
that I was always meant to be.

For I will not sit idly by
and let my life just happen.
I choose to live my life on purpose.
I choose to live with passion.

I will laugh and I will love
and sing and dance and play.
And enjoy the blessings that come
with the dawning of each new day.

Yes, here I am. Here I stand,
stating my heart's true desire:
Instead of merely living,
I will choose to Live Inspired.

STRETCH YOUR MIND

AWAKEN

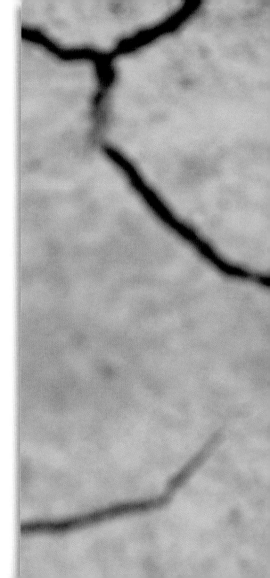

Living inspired means living with a heightened sense of awareness. Awareness of the little things as well as the big that come along — a wildflower growing on the roadside to a kindness performed in my behalf to a new opportunity. Each day there are many things that if noticed increase the beauty and joy in life.

Cindi Orr
Thatcher, Arizona

Often we find ourselves living our lives in such a way that we do not take the time to awaken our senses to the world around us. When we live unengaged and uninspired, we miss out on many of the little gifts that life presents us: a smile from a stranger, a beautiful rainbow, or the sound of a child's laughter. The point of life is not to merely stumble along, but to engage in all that life has to offer. When going about your day, why not choose to awaken to the world around you? Smell the flavorful aromas, trace a rock's edge with your finger, listen as the wind rustles the leaves, and watch as a new day unfolds before your eyes.

As each day unfolds before my eyes, I strive daily to be awake. At the age of twelve, I was diagnosed with narcolepsy, a sleep disorder characterized by excessive daytime sleepiness affecting one in two thousand people. Narcolepsy is caused by the brain's inability to regulate sleep-wake cycles normally. With sleep invading my day and wakefulness invading my night, I am often caught in this relentless haze of perpetual drowsiness. I am cognizant of the lighting in the room, my stress level (too much emotion brings on cataplexy—sudden muscle weakness), my caffeine intake, what I eat, and my exercise level. During those periods when my narcolepsy is worse, I often have a difficult time awakening my senses to the world around me. Feeling unbearably sleepy, I wake up in the morning after a full night's sleep only to need a nap two hours later. A fellow narcoleptic commented that he was awake at 1 a.m. for the first time all day. Such is the life of the narcoleptic: searching for what stimulates us, what flips the "awake" switch, what keeps us from falling asleep. While staying awake, alert, and focused requires daily effort, I'm able to function quite well by arranging my work schedule, asking for help when I need it, taking regular naps, and exercising.

While I can get frustrated at times, I am grateful for my narcolepsy. Because of it, I do not take being alert for granted. Each moment that I'm full of life, vigor, and vitality, I count as a blessing. When my eyes are opened and sleep feels far away I delight in my surroundings. I smell the air after the fresh rain. Touch the face of my sweet child. See the light as it spills in through the window.

I want you to begin this inspired journey by awakening your senses to the world around you. Take a deep breath. Relish in the beauty that today has brought. What sensations do you notice? How do you feel? Use the page at the end of this chapter to write what you discover as you awaken to your surroundings.

True awareness of our surroundings and our capacities within it. To be reawoken to our possibilities. To live more engaged, richer lives as a result of all this consciousness. This is living an inspired life.

Estrella Levy
Rockville, Maryland

Whether the dawn is darkened with the trials and tribulations of life or suffused with the brilliance of joys, it is the tiny nuances of life that should keep us going: for me inspiration and meaning in life come from the seemingly mundane: a baby's toothless smile; a mother's nurturing; a lover's caress; a bird's melodious twitter; the wind whistling through the trees amidst the mayhem on the streets below; a child's implicit faith, innocence, and trust in everything. All this and more is rejuvenation for the soul and succor for the spirit to go on.

Swati Kiran

Bangalore, Karnataka, India

Living inspired means so much more to me now than ever. I am a breast cancer survivor. I have a life, and never a day goes by when I don't think of how lucky I am to enjoy all the things that life has to offer. Like the rain and the snow and the sleet and the sun shining. I love it all. It all makes me feel alive!

Lift your head when you go outside and remember that if you can feel the sun on your face or the rain gets you wet or you are cold, then you are alive...and that's a great feeling!

Sherrie Carroll

Windsor, California

WHEN I AWAKEN MY SENSES TO THE WORLD AROUND ME, I FIND...

EXPLORE

I wake up every morning and I say "Yes!" to life, for the air is crisp, the flowers are fresh, and the birds are singing. The same power which enlivens those beautiful creatures can empower me today. For the same power which gives breath to men and a song to the birds will give me the power to achieve. This inspires me day after day...after day, to reach for the future, with hope.

Judith Brown-Foster
St. Catherine, Jamaica

Each day is a blessed day and waking up in the morning is another day to look forward to and to explore and to learn new or different aspects of what life has to offer.

Nafisah Ali

Kuala Lumpur, Malaysia

What would make men walk 2,000 miles barefoot? Or travel by sailboat to an unknown land? Or leave their homes and families to risk the chance to die because of harsh conditions?

When news spread that James Marshall had discovered gold on John Sutter's land in January of 1848, the California Gold Rush began. Inspired by the prospect of a new life, many risked life and limb to travel the journey. Between the years of 1848 and 1855, 300,000 men, women, and children traveled to California to try their hands at earning a fortune. While most to arrive in California were Americans, gold-seekers came from places as far away as Latin America, Asia, Europe, and Australia. These determined men, women, and children risked their lives to explore uncharted terrain all because they were inspired to achieve their dreams.

If we are to live inspired, it's important to know what touches each of us. We must know what gets our blood flowing; what makes our feet want to hit the floor running; what makes us tick. We must explore our own hearts and discover what would make us want to *cross rivers, climb mountains, wade through water, traverse the plains, and sail across oceans,* so to speak.

Since we're all made differently, we respond to life in different ways. The same passage in a book might bring on sleepiness for one person yet give goose bumps to another. A single song may be considered loud noise to one yet invigorating music to another. An afternoon alone may bore one person yet rejuvenate another. Phil Cousineau in his book *Stoking the Creative Fires* writes, "When asked what inspires me, I say, 'Whatever sets my soul on fire.' That means travel, books, art, music, photography, nature, or cafe conversation."

What inspires you? What brings you the most energy? Where do you feel most alive? In what settings do you flourish? What time of day do you feel most enlightened? Look into the depths of your soul and examine what *sets your soul on fire*.

Enthused by the dawn of a new day.
Stimulated by someone's smile.
Moved by the sound of laughter.
Stirred to take another step forward
even if it appears to be a challenge.
Encouraged to live fully with simplicity.
Motivated by the love of my son.
Inspired to "Walk my Talk" via the Inspired Living Cafe.

Susan van der Rassel
North Bay, Ontario, Canada

Living inspired means that each morning when I open my curtains to the beautiful African sun, I know that my goals for the day will be accomplished. The sun is like a good friend, always there, even if behind a cloud for a few brief hours. Knowing this gives me the vitality to live the day with purpose and integrity.

Theresa Stolk

Gauteng, South Africa

WHAT SETS MY SOUL ON FIRE...

DREAM

Living inspired means always keeping your mind open to possibilities.

Elaine Carr Spain
Montgomery, Alabama

I knew I would like her instantly. Spunky in spirit, inspiring in tone, Lisa Hammond is a force to be reckoned with. Lisa's book *Dream Big* was the first book that I read for the Inspired Living Cafe. I remember reading the book out in my mom and dad's hammock. It was one of those days where everything just seemed *blah*. Page after page, her humor and wit inspired me. I was impressed by her tenacity, uplifted by her story, and the deeper I went into the book, the lighter my heart felt. I was smiling, I was relaxing, I was enjoying the beautiful day. I got online to check out more about this woman and company that I had just read about and saw that she was having a workshop in San Francisco. Immediately, I called my friend Kelley and told her that we had to attend the workshop. I wanted to be inspired, I wanted to be around the excitement. We decided to invite our moms and four months later, there we were, having lunch with Lisa Hammond.

Lisa wasn't always the founder of the wildly successful Femail Creations. She hasn't always been the CEO of a company dedicated to empowering and inspiring women. She was once working out of a two-room home office, managing the office side of the construction company with her husband who was managing the field side. But she was a woman with a passion for others. And a dream to spend her days doing meaningful work.

For a decade, Lisa filled notebooks with ideas in her what-do-I-want-to-be-when-I-grow-up journal. These newspaper clippings, pictures, and scribbled thoughts became the seeds that eventually led to *Femail Creations: Gifts to Celebrate and Inspire*. Her mail-order catalog company focuses on supporting women artists and other women-owned businesses. The company gives back to the community by highlighting a different charity of focus in each catalog. Lisa has made a difference in the lives of women around the world because she chose to dream big.

What is that dream, deep down in your heart, that you long to have fulfilled? Maybe you'd like to pick up a new hobby or learn a new language. Maybe your dream is to travel to some distant land, or visit a nearby town. Maybe you've always wanted to teach others or own your own business. Or maybe right now, you only have a seed of a dream. Wherever you are, take time now to answer the question, "What is your dream?" Don't hold back. Go ahead and *dream big*.

Awaken every day to follow your dream.

Mark Malinowski

Chicago, Illinois

We all have someone or something that inspires us; something that spurs us on to reach for our dreams and goals. Living inspired means to wake each day stimulated and enthusiastic about being one step closer to that goal and what the day will bring.

Doreen Novotny
Orange, California

Living inspired means living with passion in everything you do, living with a great purpose in mind.

Amy Lawrence

Roseville, California

My dream is...

LISTEN

Living inspired is a call to rise above the
mundane. It's going forward
and reaching out. It's having ears
to hear what is being said in the heavenlies
and grabbing hold of it
for today.

Eve Kline Evans
Albrightsville, Pennsylvania

To me living inspired means living in tune to the Spirit, listening to that still, small voice, so you can make the best choices and decisions.

Sue Cline

Waukee, Iowa

Life coach Carolyn Himes had been working through a motivational program with her clients. On week four, the focus was geared toward physical health and taking care of things that we all have a tendency to procrastinate with. Realizing that she shouldn't introduce tools to others that she herself didn't utilize or follow through on, she knew that she needed to make an appointment for her annual physical exam, an exam that she had not had in two years. Her mind told her, "You feel great. You don't have any symptoms. Plus, you don't have health insurance and you know how costly exams can be. This can wait."

Days later, Carolyn sat working alone in her garden, prepping the soil to plant new bulbs for spring. As she was working, her flip flop got stuck and she landed in the dirt with a thud. When she fell, she heard the words echo throughout her body, "Don't wait. This appointment is important." She listened to that inner voice and decided to take action. That moment in the garden gave her confirmation that, in fact, she should not wait.

She went to the appointment and within a week received the test results. They indicated that she needed further testing. After those results came back, she was able to ask for additional testing, and off she went for round three. To get herself back on track while she waited for the outcome, she reached out for tools and found Fran Drescher's book *Cancer Schmancer*. Here, she found answers, hope, and ways to take action.

Then the call came, "Hi, Carolyn, we are saving the last appointment today for you. Please come in. The doctor would like to speak with you." It was this day that she realized her inner knowing is present and is there to help her and others. She was diagnosed with cervical cancer. Friends and family pulled together for her and she was able to have the needed surgery and aftercare.

One year later, a cancer-free Carolyn participated in the Revlon Run/Walk for Women in Los Angeles and was able to thank Fran Drescher in person for being an inspiration. As Carolyn says, "We need to share our stories. They may just save a life."

Take a moment. Be still and quiet. What might that voice of discernment be saying to you?

Living inspired means living through your heart and listening to it.

Evonne Hawe

Butte, Montana

Inspired living to me means recognizing the joy and love that is present in any moment and situation, even and especially in the challenging ones!

Shelly Rachanow
Laguna Niguel, California

WHEN I LISTEN TO MY INNER VOICE, I HEAR...

_____

_____

_____

_____

_____

_____

_____

_____

_____

_____

_____

_____

GLADDEN YOUR HEART

SING

Living inspired causes me to rejoice as I am filled with the wonder of creation's colors all around me.

Shirley Alexander
Fergus, Ontario, Canada

Renew your mind with thoughts of greatness, passion for others and continued hopefulness of humanity.

Victoria Quintana

Murrieta, California

Sing. Sing a song. Sing out loud. Sing out strong. Sing of good things, not bad. Sing of happy, not sad. Are you with me, Sesame Street aficionados? When I was a child, I would sing. Sing a song. I'd sing out loud. I'd sing out strong. And when I got to the *la la la la la's,* there was no stopping me. As an adult, I know that I'm not the greatest singer. In fact, I'm really a terrible singer. But I still love to sing.

I've noticed that when I'm living uninspired, I'm often quiet as I go about my day. There's no song, no melody in my head. What's missing is my song. That literal song that makes me smile. That song that makes me feel like a kid again. When my song is missing, I'm often worried. Or stressed out. Or tired. About a year ago, my song had been missing for a few weeks. Maybe even months. I did not even realize it at the time. As I was washing dishes one afternoon I heard it. I was singing out loud. All by myself, not a care in the world. At that moment, my spirit had been set free and I was living inspired.

Since then, I've realized that when I nourish my soul with what matters most to me, time spent with family, doing meaningful work, or activities that are positive for my mind, body, and spirit, sure enough, my song returns. My song wants to be sung. My song wants to be set free.

What is your song? Whether it's a literal song, or some other form of self-expression, set it free. You'll be amazed at how your heart will smile. Maya Angelou says, "A bird doesn't sing because it has an answer, it sings because it has a song." So go ahead and sing. Sing a song.

Living inspired is a day to day process. I find when I am most inspired I am involved somehow in a nice circle of inspiration. Inspired, I can continue my work inspiring others, creating a circle of inspiration that can continue to flow.

Danny Freedman
Edmonton, Alberta, Canada

Living inspired to me means finding pleasure in the little things: my baby grandson's smile, thanks and appreciation from my patients, that look from my husband that says I love you—without him saying a word, the feel of the sun on my face, being truly thankful for every day I have on this earth.

Sandy Gray
Wichita, Kansas

Rejoice in the moment!
Rejoicing in each and every moment, regardless of what it is,
is a positive and invigorating aspect of our human ability to
nourish our spiritual being.

Sister Catherine D.M. Yaskiw
Toronto, Ontario, Canada

MY SONG THAT LONGS TO BE SET FREE...

DANCE

Living inspired means living every moment with an openness and freshness, expecting the unexpected and finding unimaginable wealth and joy in the simple things of life.

Germaine Jacob
Ste. Rose, Manitoba, Canada

On that fateful day, my husband and I were staying in a hotel in Portland, Oregon, our "home" for six weeks. After the early morning phone call alerting us to the tragedy, we sat, as those all over the world, in shock as we watched the events unfolding before us on the morning of September 11th, 2001. Alone in a new city, trying to gather our bearings, we lived the next few days in a fog. I felt guilty for laughing. After all, *How could I be happy when so much sadness had befallen my fellow Americans?*

Alone during the day while my husband worked, I navigated this new city by myself. The city was nice enough, but it was not my city. The people were friendly enough, but these were not my people. I was in a different place, surrounded by strangers, as questions of security, stability, and the meaning of life flooded my mind. In this adopted city, the shows of patriotism were overwhelming. Flags were hung outside of buildings. People gathered for candlelight vigils. As a group, we were searching for meaning as the events replayed over and over in our minds. Adults all over the city were concerned. A change had taken place. Times were now different.

One afternoon, as I was walking around the city, I sat on a park bench. The somber mood of the city, and of the entire nation, weighed heavily on my mind. Holding my head in my hands, I began to cry for those lost. When I opened my eyes, I saw her. A young girl, probably five or six, dancing in an outdoor fountain. Seeing the smile on her face, the joy in her movements, my heart began to gladden. I was filled with a sense of calm, of well-being, of knowing that things would be okay. Here, this darling child before me was not burdened. She did not worry for her safety. She was not overwhelmed with sadness. Instead, with her childlike wonder, she was laughing, and dancing, basking in the beautiful day. This was the moment when I saw hope. Hope for our lives and hope for our nation.

It's possible that when you're feeling free and unburdened, your first reaction isn't to dance. But picture a time when you've felt like this precious child dancing in the fountain; when you've felt light, uninhibited, inspired. I want you to describe that feeling. There is a Hopi Indian saying that says, "To watch us dance is to hear our hearts speak." When you "dance," what does your heart say?

Living inspired is to live knowing that who you are is enough and to feel authentic and empowered from within, regardless of external circumstances.

Loren M. Gelberg-Goff
River Edge, New Jersey

Living inspired means you have found your purpose in life.
When you are on purpose all things are viewed in a positive manner.

Dr. Robert Buchla
Plano, Illinois

I believe to be inspired is to be indwelled with a power beyond myself. To be inspired is to become someone greater and more loving than I am without that inspiration. I believe that to be inspired enables me to be more creative in doing the tasks that are before me.

Zintka O. Bilyeu

Decatur, Illinois

WHEN I'M INSPIRED, MY HEART SAYS…

MOVE

Living inspired means living a life of peace and joy and helping to maintain a healthy way of living; being good to yourself as well as others. Life can really be great if you let it!

Linda Lorraine Dennis
Norfolk, Virginia

Living inspired to me means living with the knowledge that what I do or fail to do today really matters.

Bill Henwood

Norman, Oklahoma

Imagine if you knew that tomorrow, you'd no longer have the use of your legs. Today, would you choose to sit, or would you fill the day with running, jumping, skipping, and leaping? I bet you'd be out there working up a sweat, taking advantage of the body that you have been given. Why is it, then, that we find ourselves sitting when we have the capacity to get in motion? Why do we wonder why we've gained a few pounds if we're not moving in our daily lives? Why do we wonder why have weight-related diseases if we haven't treated our bodies properly? After giving it some thought, the answers seem pretty obvious.

There is one girl who is using exercise to inspire the world. With a heart for those around her, Sarah runs to inspire others, especially the next generation coming up, to get into motion. Her motto is, "I wake up every day asking myself, 'How can my life be a blessing to some one, some way, some how, some where?'" When I asked ultramarathoner Sarah Stanley why she runs, she said, "I run fifty or one hundred miles to inspire someone to run or walk one mile." While she knows that most of us aren't anywhere near the level that she's at, she says, "I know you can get outside and take a one-mile walk or run." Sarah is on a mission to make the world healthy, fit, and happy...one person at a time. And through her company Sarah Stanley Inspired, she's using her races and her life as inspiration. "When you exercise," she says, "you will find that your daily life will be better."

Running might not be right for you. Maybe you enjoy walking or biking or swimming. Maybe pilates or yoga or dance classes are more your style. Maybe it's racquetball or tennis or golf. Maybe it's even taking the stairs rather than the elevator, or choosing a far spot in the parking lot. The world is filled with ways to get, and stay, in motion. Do what works for you. Really, can you afford not to? Consider the quote of Edward Stanley, British statesman in the 1800s, who said, "Those who think they have not time for bodily exercise will sooner or later have to find time for illness."

Exercise is a vital part of the mind-body-spirit connection, and one way to live an inspired life is to make staying in motion an integral part of our lives. Taking care of our bodies is an essential part of *living inspired.* Find what you enjoy...and move.

Inspired living is wholesome motivation of the body and soul by doing things that interest you most.

Rutendo Nyoni

Harare, Zimbabwe

Feel the glory in the opportunity to walk in your own shoes, for no one else can do that as well as you can. Be thankful for this day, for another one is not promised to you. Let your heart be an inspiration to another—you might just start a ripple effect.
Above all, be true to yourself: you have to file this day away in your own personal history book.

Debra Coleman
Lebanon, Virginia

Inspired living means to live your best. To live in the moment but yet earn for the future. To reach for it and to never look back. To always remain positive, to give freely and to love always.
Enjoy the ride and the moments.

Jennifer Metzger
Elmira, Ontario, Canada

WAYS I CAN STAY IN MOTION...

RELINQUISH

*Living inspired means
to accept the past for what it was
and embrace the future for what it will be
based on what we do today.*

Darcy Latta
Regina, Saskatchewan
Canada

My father worked as a Special Agent for the US Department of the Treasury for twenty-five years before retiring. He is a detail-oriented perfectionist who takes pride in his work. When I was a child, he spent many hours at the office, most days leaving at six a.m. and coming home around midnight. I saw him on the weekends, but he was usually catching up on sleep. At the time, this was normal to me: I was young, my mother was tons of fun, and I really didn't know any other way.

When I was nine years old, things changed. During this time, the pace and intensity of my father's life came crashing down. Late one evening, an older colleague told him, "This can wait. Do you know what happens after you finish this case? There will be another one. Slow down. You'll burn yourself out." Those words hit home.

Upon rebuilding his life and restructuring his time, a new father emerged. One who I saw in the evenings, who played Monopoly, and who took me to play miniature golf. It was this dad who had heart-to-heart talks with me as he cooked our dinner, who sat down with me and did math problems, and who provided a safe place by letting me crawl up into his lap.

My father chose to restructure his life in such a way that would include those things that matter most. I'm so thankful that he listened to those wise words spoken so many years ago. Those words changed my father's heart, and ultimately my life...

"This can wait. Slow down."

To make room for new goals, new behaviors, or a new way of living, we must choose to get rid of some of the old. When our spirit is filled with emotions, to-do lists, and self-defeating behaviors, there is no room for anything else. What is holding you back from becoming that person that you are meant to be? What things can you let go of? What counterproductive beliefs do you need to relinquish? Maybe it's the idea that you need to be a perfect spouse, parent, or friend. Maybe you need to remove an obligation or two that's overwhelming you. Maybe it's a memory from the past that continues to weigh you down. What is it that you need to relinquish in order to live inspired?

Living inspired means approaching each day as an adventure to learn, uncover, resolve, or move beyond.

Charlotte Elder

Lilburn, Georgia

Inspired living means you accept responsibility for your life by consciously making choices to ensure that you feel the best that you possibly can, in each moment, as you reach out to experience life to its fullest.

Jenny Wern

Lake Havasu City, Arizona

Surround yourself, your life, your job,
your ideas, your free time, your sleep time
with things you love.
Leave no room for anything else.
Be thankful for all of it!
The rest will take care of itself.

Pat Holley

Beech Island, South Carolina

I CAN RELINQUISH...

NOURISH YOUR SOUL

RISK

Everyone has challenges, but you have to take those challenges and turn them into assets. Embrace your passions. Get out of your comfort zone and do the thing you wouldn't ordinarily do. You will then be drawn into living inspired.

Tom H. Netherton
Litchfield Park, Arizona

Living inspired is waking up excited about the gift of today!
When you live inspired, there's always a gift!

Vicki Williams

Albany, Georgia

As he dressed in the morning, preparing for the journey ahead, he put on two pair of socks, two pair of underwear, two pair of pants, two shirts, a sweater and a jacket. Carrying a suitcase would arouse suspicion. After grabbing his bag, filled with schoolbooks, he kissed his mother goodbye and started for the front door. Standing in the doorway, he glanced back at his house...one last time. The date was April 6, 1956, his eighteenth birthday, and the day that Peter Schladitz would escape from East Germany.

In this moment, Peter took the first of many steps. Steps that would take him to a Berlin-bound train, steps that would take him to a subway ride from East to West Germany, and steps that would take him to freedom. Taking this first step set the wheels in motion. As an eighteen-year-old, raised in a rural town, navigating Berlin's city streets all alone would have been a daunting task, even under the best of circumstances. When he entered the city on this day, he knew that one wrong move could cost him his life.

While he sat aboard the subway train, he froze as the Russian guards patrolled up and down the aisle. After managing to keep his composure, because his life depended on it, he eventually walked out of the subway station. It was then that he kissed the ground. Peter escaped communist oppression and is now living the life of his dreams because he took a risk.

Most of us will never be faced with the need to flee our homelands. But we can all take risks that will help us get closer to living the lives of our dreams. Maybe it's taking a new job, or taking a stand on an important issue. Maybe it's speaking out for someone who doesn't have a voice or speaking up for yourself. What risks do you need to take so that you may live inspired?

When I live most of every hour, filled with the love of my family, filled with the fascination of discovering new things to create, and filled with the joy of being alive, I am living inspired.

Karen Eugene
Alexandria, Indiana

Living inspired means that I am living with the understanding that life begins when opportunity comes. Each moment is an opportunity for me to embrace life and all of its joys. I am learning each day to understand that a purposeful life is one that is fully lived! And it is only when you come to this powerful realization that you are responsible for you that this small yet powerful revelation will inspire you to live your best life.

Ann-Marie Moulton
Toronto, Canada

Living inspired is a choice—and what a great choice it is. I will always choose to live inspired rather than live uninspired. It is the difference between contentment and disappointment and I choose contentment. If I am lacking a tool, I will go get it; if I am lacking a skill, I will learn it; if I am lacking companionship, I will make a friend; if I am lacking motivation, I will remember hope. I choose to live inspired!

Elizabeth Griffin
Larned, Kansas

Risks I can take which may lead me to live more inspired...

RISE

Living inspired doesn't mean that life is perfect—quite the contrary! Living inspired means that, even while in the midst of personal or business-related turmoil, I am grateful not for material things, but for simple things like the ability to love and be loved. Living inspired means feeling blessed for things that most of us take advantage of every day: the gift of eyesight, hearing, voice, touch...Living inspired is the feeling of blessing even when things in my day don't seem to be going my way. Living inspired is a choice.

Jenny Magallanes
San Diego, California

During the first holiday season that the Inspired Living Cafe was open, we held a contest to find the Welcome The Rain Woman, based on my book *Welcome The Rain: Choosing to See Beyond Life's Storms.* We were looking for the woman who we felt had handled her storms with the most style and grace. The Inspired Living Cafe community came together and over 800 submissions poured in from all over the world. The day came when we needed to make our final decision, which proved to be an extremely difficult task. On this day, we gathered around the conference room table and after Lynne's story had been read aloud, the moment lingered as we sat in silence, wiping our tears. We all knew that this was the story that needed to be told.

Here is the submission that her husband, Rick, sent us:

"Lynne and I lost our youngest daughter Ashley around Thanksgiving time 2007 in a single car crash just a couple of miles from home. Lynne has been struggling with such a great loss, but has not skipped a beat in caring for our other two children, the home and work. Our oldest child was born with cerebral palsy and requires constant attention. In addition to the loss of Ashley, Lynne lost her mother this year as well. Although it has been hard she has become involved in 'Gift of Life' organ and tissue donation, setting up a memorial scholarship honoring Ashley, and consoling her best friend after she

lost her sister. I know each day it hurts because on Lynne's way to work she passes the crash site that bears the scars not only on the tree Ashley hit, but the scars in her heart, and I know it opens that wound each time she goes by. Lynne is a great girl, I thank God for her, I know she deserves a spot in Heaven…"

How does a parent rise again after losing a child? As unimaginable as this can seem, this is a reality that Lynne and Rick have lived with. Not only has she risen, but she has cared for and helped others with kindness and compassion. Lynne, a lovely and humble woman replied, "It is not only me that should be honored but all the women in this world who have made a difference in someone's life no matter how large or small it may be." The way Lynne handled her storms with such style and grace while focusing on others is an inspiration to us all.

When you fall, where can you find strength? Where can you put your focus? What inspires you to rise again?

Living inspired is knowing that service to others is the greatest benefit to oneself. By giving of oneself, we receive multiple tangible and intangible rewards in our lives.

Darryl G. Chatman
Richmond, Texas

Living inspired means that I live in a state of perpetual gratitude. I am grateful for my life, for each new day, for my family, friends and associates, for the ability to love and be loved. I am grateful for my career as a Nurse Practitioner, for the ability to touch people's lives and be touched by their lives. I am grateful for my daily meals, shelter and clothing, for my freedom of speech, and for being able to become the person that God created me to be.

Evelyn Haughton

Bronx, New York

Inspired living is waking up each day with a sense of purpose to create a good day versus expect a good day. I make a conscious and concerted effort to plant positive seeds to generate the inspiration I need to refuel my mind, body, and spirit to keep me moving onward and upward. Inspiration comes from within. I'm blessed that it burns brightly in my heart giving me a calming focus to inspire others in my journey of life.

Rita Suiter
Valdosta, Georgia

WHAT INSPIRES ME TO RISE AGAIN WHEN THINGS ARE TOUGH…

BLESS

We hear so much about living a life of purpose, which is all well and good. But if your purpose is all about you and your self-centered focus, then that purpose is less than ideal. If your purpose is about a life of service to those around you, then that's inspired living.

Richard Hamilton
Brea, California

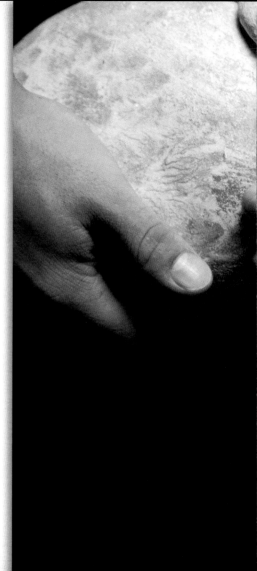

Start each day with the intention of doing something good for someone else.
It gives you a purpose and a sense of accomplishment.

Lyn Reynolds,

Spring, Texas

The Austin Chronicle writes, "Stephens feels she's blessed to have her cafe open, but trust us: Austin diners are the ones who are blessed." "Stephens" is Lola Stephens, founder of Nubian Queen Lola's Cajun Kitchen. A Louisiana native, Lola settled into Austin, Texas, in the early 1980s. By the late eighties, she had lost her job as a cashier and found herself homeless for two years. She fought back and thus began the ride of her life.

In 2004, Lola stumbled across a small cafe that was for rent. Growing up learning how to cook from her mother, owning her own cafe was a dream come true. With donations from her church, she was able to pay for one month's rent. Inspired by Joseph's coat of many colors and Mardi Gras, she decorated and painted the cafe herself in bright colors. Three months later, she still didn't have enough money to open the place. Because of the generosity of a contractor, who took her on a $1,000-plus shopping spree, she was able to finally open her doors.

She blesses those in her community by closing on Sundays so that she can feed the local homeless in the cafe's back yard for free. After the floods in Louisiana, she organized several benefits for the displaced. She also volunteered and cooked for them at a shelter.

While life has taken Lola down a long, bumpy road, she is living an inspired life by blessing those around her.

Think of some of the talents that you've been given. How can you allow your talents to help others? How can you give of your other resources such as time and money? How can you be a blessing to those around you?

Inspired Living to me means being positive when things are not right in your world. Helping others to face their problems in a positive way and just be a role model for those who could use someone positive in their lives. Inspired living means making the best of what the world has to offer and giving that back to other people.

Chris Binek
United States

Passion is contagious and when you have the courage to share your passion for life with those around you it can inspire others to find the path to their dreams!

Michele DeVille

Minneapolis, Minnesota

Living inspired is having the energy and passion for something—or many things—which focuses your energy, your thoughts, and gives purpose to each day. To be vital and involved is to be inspired to make life the best it can be for you and for those around you.

Vicki Simons
Wahoo, Nebraska

WAYS THAT I CAN BLESS OTHERS...

SHINE

To live inspired is to continuously remember that you were created for a special purpose.

Lupe Reesman
Tucson, Arizona

When you are able to get yourself into alignment with who you really are, you feel inspired, you feel motivated, confident, and excited. In this state, we can accomplish anything our hearts desire.

Jennifer Carter

Goodview, Virginia

Friendly in nature, athletic at heart, spunky in spirit. She has the presence that can light up a room. Open, inviting, and energetic, she lives life passionately. But at 250 pounds, living passionately was draining. Unable to participate in the activities she once enjoyed, she found herself living a rather sedentary life. After a conversation with her housepainter, who, after seeking help, was able to lose a great deal of weight, she, too, got help. After a year of making her own health a priority, she had lost 100 pounds.

She is now able to keep up with her grandkids, bike, run, swim, and teach racquetball classes at the local junior college. Her energy is endless. With a heart for others, she now has the energy to volunteer for Meals on Wheels, Care Corps, where she drives the elderly to doctors' appointments, and is a greeter at the airport.

No longer restricted by her size, she takes on each day with passion—thankful to be around to enjoy her family, blessed to live her charmed life, grateful for her newfound freedom. *She* is my mother, and she has become that person whom she always wanted to be: *one who lives inspired.*

This past year, my mom and I competed in a triathlon together. This race was a celebration of victory over her hard-fought battle to lose weight. While seasoned triathletes would laugh at our race times, to us, our times didn't matter. In our heart of hearts, we know that we accomplished so much. We competed in the race. We finished. More importantly, she competed. She finished. At the end of the triathlon, my mother, who two years before couldn't have walked around the block without tiring out, held my hand as we crossed the finish line together. The expression on her face was priceless—it was a moment unlike any other. When we are true to ourselves, we can then live inspired; living life as we were meant to be.

It's now time to discover what it means for you personally to live inspired. Who is that person, deep down inside of you, who wants to come out? Seek out that true, authentic person that you are meant to be. What does your inspired self act like? feel like? talk like? I want you to describe your inspired self. Who is the person who longs to be free?

Living inspired is a state of mind that you choose. When you find your 'zone of creativity' and create a vision, each day takes on new meaning. This allows you to wake up each morning energized, from knowing you have the opportunity to make strides toward your goals. You are eager and willing to step out and act on your convictions and ideals. You are pursuing your passions with enthusiasm and excitement. When you operate in your 'zone of creativity' others cannot help but catch that enthusiasm. You become a beacon of inspiration to others as you pursue your dreams.

Lisa Schilling
Trenton, Missouri

Living inspired is living in a state of constant creativity. Never feeling like I am finished, or perfected, but excited to keep growing toward a greater degree of satisfaction and happiness. To offer encouraging thoughts to myself and others so that I won't be judging others, for that is not my purpose. To be able to learn from others, to see the good in them, and expand on these qualities would benefit everyone. Living inspired is not wasting time or money on what doesn't nourish me or others. Living in this constant state of creative energy gives more life to me and those who are around me. I then have peace and energy because I am not striving for anything but who I am created to be.

Laura Wiederspan
Fort Morgan, Colorado

My inspired self is...

CLOSING THOUGHTS

Thank you for taking this inspired journey along with me. It seems as though we must say goodbye for now. I do hope that you'll join me over at the Inspired Living Cafe (www.inspiredlivingcafe.com) where we always have something exciting brewing.

It is my hope that our time together today has been well-spent and that you feel one step closer to living the life of your dreams. Despite whatever comes your way, may you always choose a life full of love and laughter; excitement and exhilaration; happiness and hope. May you always choose to *live inspired*.

Michelle Sedas

About The Publisher

WALKTHETALK.COM

Resources for Personal and Professional Success

For over 30 years, WalkTheTalk.com has been dedicated to one simple goal…one single mission: ***To provide you and your organization with high-impact resources for your personal and professional success.***

Walk The Talk resources are designed to:
- Develop your skills and confidence
- Inspire your team
- Create customer enthusiasm
- Build leadership skills
- Stretch your mind
- Handle tough "people problems"
- Develop a culture of respect and responsibility
- And, most importantly, help you achieve your personal and professional goals.

Contact the Walk The Talk team at
1.888.822.9255
or visit us at www.walkthetalk.com.

ABOUT THE AUTHOR

Michelle Sedas is the author of the best-selling books *Welcome The Rain* and *Live Inspired*. She is the coauthor of *The Power of 10%*. As the host of the Inspired Living Cafe (www.inspiredlivingcafe.com), Michelle writes on themes intended to *stretch your mind*, *gladden your heart*, and *nourish your soul*. You can also find Michelle at www.michellesedas.com.

Visit WalkTheTalk.com to learn more about our:

Leadership and Employee Development Centre
• Develop your Leaders
• Build Employee Commitment
• Achieve Business Results

NEW Walk The Talk Digital Resources on Demand
• Immediately access information
• Over 50 "how-to" topics
• Fast and user-friendly

Motivational Gift Books
• Inspire your Team
• Create Customer Enthusiasm
• Reinforce Core Values

Free Newsletters including:
• My Daily Inspiration
• The Power of Inspiration
• Inspired Living

Be sure to order additional copies of Live Inspired!

There are two versions of *Live Inspired!*

Traditional Book $12.95   *Digital E-Book $10.95*

Better yet, order the **Live Inspired** Motivational Kit!

ONLY $29.95!

The Kit contains 3 best-selling books by Michelle Sedas:

• Welcome The Rain - Choosing To See Beyond Life's Storms

• The Power of 10% - How Small Changes Can Make a BIG Difference

• Live Inspired - Stretch Your Mind, Gladden Your Heart, Nourish Your Soul